بسم الله الرحمن الرحيم

أمثلة الحياة الدنيا

Parables

of The Life of This World

Excerpts from ‘Uddat as-Sābirīn

By

Imām Ibn al-Qayyim

رحمه الله

1445 A.H./2024 C.E. Islamic Reminders Publications

First Edition: Dhūl Qi'dah 1445 A.H./May 2024 C.E

ISBN: 979-8-32-589503-6

Title: Parables of The Life of This World – Excerpts from 'Uddat as-Sābirīn

Author: Imām Ibn al-Qayyim

Translators: Abū Ismā'īl Muṣṭafá ibn George DeBerry

Editing & Formatting: IRP Editing Team

Email: Islamicreminders1@gmail.com

Cover Art: Usūl Design

Transliteration Table

Arabic Letter	Roman	Name	Arabic Letter	Roman	Name
ا آ	ʾ / ā / * / **	ʾalif	ط	ṭ	ṭāʾ
ب	b	bāʾ	ظ	ẓ	ẓāʾ
ت	t	tāʾ	ع	ʿ	ʿayn
ث	th	thāʾ	غ	gh	ghayn
ج	j	jīm	ف	f	fāʾ
ح	ḥ	ḥāʾ	ق	q	qāf
خ	kh	khāʾ	ك	k	kāf
د	d	dāl	ل	l	lām
ذ	dh	dhāl	م	m	mīm
ر	r	rāʾ	ن	n	nūn
ز	z	zāy	ة / ه	h / t /***	tāʾ / hāʾ/ta marbūṭah
س	s	sīn	و	w / ū	wāw
ش	sh	shīn	ي	y / ī	yāʾ
ص	ṣ	ṣād	ى	á	alif maqṣūrah
ض	ḍ	ḍād			

Glyphs & Abbreviations

صَلَّى ٱللَّهُ عَلَيْهِ وَسَلَّمَ	May the Peace and Blessings of Allāh be upon him
رَضِيَ ٱللَّهُ عَنْهُ	May Allāh be pleased with him
رَضِيَ ٱللَّهُ عَنْهَا	May Allāh be pleased with her
رَضِيَ ٱللَّهُ عَنْهُمَا	May Allāh be pleased with them both
رَحِمَهُ ٱللَّهُ	May Allāh have mercy upon him
T.N.	Translator's Note
P.N.	Publisher's Note
A.H.	Islamic Hijri Calendar

Table of Contents*

The Publisher's Preface 1

1st – The Bad Dream 8

2nd – The Ugly Woman 8

3rd – The 3 States of the Servant 9

4th – Food in the Stomach 11

5th – The Ship 12

6th – The Journey 14

7th – The Tree 15

8th – The Sea 16

9th – Spring 17

10th – The Sweet World 21

11th – The Dead Sheep 22

12th – Crossing the Ocean 23

13th – The Jar of Honey 24

14th – Scattered Seeds 24

15th – A Large Fire 25

16th – The Valley 26

* These titles were created by the translator for clarity.

17th – 2 Guests 28

18th – The Bitter Sea 29

19th – A Man and His 3 Brothers 30

20th – The King and His Palace 31

21st – The King and His City 32

22nd – The Old Garment 36

23rd – The Large Basin 38

24th – The City 38

Various (short) Parables 42

Appendix – How to Use These Parables in Various Learning Settings 44

Publisher's Preface

Among the tremendous blessings of Allāh upon His servants is His clear clarification of the religion and the affairs of life, enabling them to pursue what is good and beneficial, while avoiding what is dangerous and harmful. Allāh, the Most High, stated,

وَنَزَّلْنَا عَلَيْكَ الْكِتَابَ تِبْيَانًا لِّكُلِّ شَيْءٍ وَهُدًى
وَرَحْمَةً وَبُشْرَىٰ لِلْمُسْلِمِينَ

{We have revealed to you the Book as an explanation of all things, a guide, a mercy, and good news for those who submit.} Sūrah an-Naḥl: 89

And Allāh, the All-Knowing, said,

وَقَدْ فَصَّلَ لَكُم مَّا حَرَّمَ عَلَيْكُمْ إِلَّا مَا اضْطُرِرْتُمْ إِلَيْهِ

{He has already explained to you what He has forbidden to you—except when compelled by necessity.} Sūrah al-An'ām: 119

These verses, and many more, emphasize that Muslims are given clear guidance, sparing them the burden of creating their own religious beliefs and practices, as they are already provided this by their Merciful Lord. Consequently, believers are only tasked with adherence to this guidance if they truly seek salvation in this life and the next.

Our beloved Prophet Muhammad (ﷺ) also informed his followers of this in several narrations. From them is his statement,

إنَّه لَمْ يَكُنْ نَبِيٌّ قَبْلِي إلَّا كانَ حَقًّا عليه أَنْ يَدُلَّ أُمَّتَهُ عَلَى خَيْرِ ما يَعْلَمُهُ لهمْ، وَيُنْذِرَهُمْ شَرَّ ما يَعْلَمُهُ لهمْ

"There has never been a prophet before me except that it was incumbent upon him to guide his followers to good that he knew for them and warn them from harm that he knew for them."[1]

He (صَلَّى ٱللَّهُ عَلَيْهِ وَسَلَّمَ) also said,

إنَّهُ ليس شيءٌ يُقَرِّبُكُمْ إلى الجَنَّةِ إلَّا قد أَمَرْتُكُمْ بِهِ ، و ليس شيءٌ يُقَرِّبُكُمْ إلى النارِ إلَّا قد نَهَيْتُكُمْ عنه

"There is nothing that can get you closer to Paradise except that I have ordered you to perform it, and there is nothing that gets you closer to the Hell-fire except that I have forbade you from it."[2]

One significant clarification repeated throughout the Glorious Qur'ān and in numerous narrations in the authentic Sunnah of the Prophet Muḥammad (صَلَّى ٱللَّهُ عَلَيْهِ وَسَلَّمَ) is the admonition against the allure and deceit of the worldly life.

Allāh, the Most High, stated,

وَمَا ٱلْحَيَوٰةُ ٱلدُّنْيَآ إِلَّا لَعِبٌ وَلَهْوٌ ۖ وَلَلدَّارُ ٱلْـَٔاخِرَةُ خَيْرٌ لِّلَّذِينَ يَتَّقُونَ ۗ أَفَلَا تَعْقِلُونَ

{This worldly life is no more than play and amusement, but far better is the (eternal) Home of the Hereafter for those mindful (of Allāh).

1 Reported in *Ṣaḥīḥ Muslim* (1844)

2 Reported by *Ibn Abī Shaybah* (35473), *al-Ḥākim* (2136), and declared authentic by Shaykh al-Albānī in *Silsila as-Ṣaḥīḥa* (2866)

Will you not then understand?} Sūrah al-'An'ām: 32

And He, the All-Mighty, said,

ٱعْلَمُوٓا۟ أَنَّمَا ٱلْحَيَوٰةُ ٱلدُّنْيَا لَعِبٌ وَلَهْوٌ وَزِينَةٌ وَتَفَاخُرٌۢ بَيْنَكُمْ وَتَكَاثُرٌ فِى
ٱلْأَمْوَٰلِ وَٱلْأَوْلَـٰدِ ۖ كَمَثَلِ غَيْثٍ أَعْجَبَ ٱلْكُفَّارَ نَبَاتُهُۥ ثُمَّ يَهِيجُ فَتَرَىٰهُ
مُصْفَرًّا ثُمَّ يَكُونُ حُطَـٰمًا ۖ وَفِى ٱلْـَٔاخِرَةِ عَذَابٌ شَدِيدٌ وَمَغْفِرَةٌ مِّنَ ٱللَّهِ
وَرِضْوَٰنٌ ۚ وَمَا ٱلْحَيَوٰةُ ٱلدُّنْيَآ إِلَّا مَتَـٰعُ ٱلْغُرُورِ

{Know that this worldly life is no more than play, amusement, luxury, mutual boasting, and competition in wealth and children. This is like rain that causes plants to grow, to the delight of the planters. But later the plants dry up and you see them wither, then they are reduced to chaff. And in the Hereafter, there will be either severe punishment or forgiveness and pleasure of Allāh, whereas the life of this world is no more than the delusion of enjoyment.} Sūrah al-Ḥadīd: 20

And He, the All Mighty, said,

وَمَا هَـٰذِهِ ٱلْحَيَوٰةُ ٱلدُّنْيَآ إِلَّا لَهْوٌ وَلَعِبٌ ۚ وَإِنَّ ٱلدَّارَ
ٱلْـَٔاخِرَةَ لَهِىَ ٱلْحَيَوَانُ ۚ لَوْ كَانُوا۟ يَعْلَمُونَ

{This worldly life is no more than play and amusement. But the Hereafter is indeed the real life, if only they knew.} Sūrah al-'Ankabūt: 64

Prophet Muḥammad (ﷺ) also cautioned his nation against being ensnared by worldly pursuits.

He (ﷺ) said,

الدُّنيا مَلْعُونةٌ ، مَلْعونٌ ما فِيها ، إلا ذِكرَ اللَّهِ و ما والاه ، و عالِمًا أو مُتعلمًا

"This world, and everything in it is cursed, except for the remembrance of Allāh, what is conducive to that, the religious scholars, and seekers of knowledge."[3]

For this reason, we find that great scholars from the Salaf as-Ṣāliḥ have gone through great lengths in authoring independent books on the topic of the dangers of this worldly life, as well as extensively discussing it within their various scholarly works. From the independent and extensive works authored on this topic are:

Az-Zuhd by Abū Hātim ar-Rāzī (died 277 A.H.)

Az-Zuhd by Aḥmad bin Ḥanbal (died 241 A.H.)

Az-Zuhd by Waq'ī bin al-Jarāḥ (died 197 A.H.)

Az-Zuhd by Ibn al-Mubārak (died 181 A.H.)

Az-Zuhd by Abū Dāwūd as-Sijistānī (died 275 A.H.)

Dhum ad-Dunyā by Ibn Abī Dunyā (died 281 A.H.)

Ḥilyat al-Awliyāh by Abū Nuʿaym al-Asbahānī (died 430 A.H.)

And many other works that were authored specifically on this

3 Reported in *at-Tirmidhī* (2322), *Ibn Mājah* (4112), and graded authentic by Shaykh al-Albānī in *Ṣaḥīḥ al-Jām'* (3414)

topic.

From the scholars of Islām who have extensively discussed this topic in his various works is the great scholar and teacher Imām Ibn al-Qayyim (died 751 A.H.). If one were to read his various works, one would find that he frequently mentions the dangers of worldly life and emphasizes how crucial it is for the believer to be cautious of. One of those works is his treatise titled: *'Uddat as-Sābirīn*.[4] This book focuses on the importance of patience and gratitude in the life of the believer, and while discussing that topic, the author also presents numerous proofs illustrating the harms of the life of this world. He stated,

"The lover and admirer of the Dunyā, who prefers it over the Hereafter, is from the most foolish of creation and the most lacking in intellect, for he preferred illusion over reality, dreams over wakefulness, fleeting shade over eternal bliss, the transient abode over the everlasting home. He sold the eternal life and most comfortable living for a life that is but a dream of sleep, or a fleeting shadow. Indeed, the wise individual is not deceived by such. An Arab poet said about a people who presented him food, and he ate, then he went to the shade of a tent and slept. (While sleeping) they removed the tent, and he was struck by the sun, so he woke up, saying,

'If a man's worldly affairs are his greatest concern,
he is held by a rope of delusion.'"[5]

It is also worth mentioning that one of the remarkable ways our Lord imparts information and knowledge in His Holy Qur'ān is through parables and examples, as these aid individuals in reflecting on and understanding the messages being conveyed.

---

4 The Arabic edition used for this translation was Dār 'Ālim al-Fawāid, 1st edition the year 1429 A.H.
5 *'Uddat as-Sābirīn* pg. 435

Allāh, the Most High, states,

وَتِلْكَ الْأَمْثَالُ نَضْرِبُهَا لِلنَّاسِ ۖ وَمَا يَعْقِلُهَا إِلَّا الْعَالِمُونَ

{And We present these examples for mankind, but none will understand them except those who have knowledge (of Allāh).} Sūrah al-'Ankabūt: 43

And He, the All-Knowing, stated,

وَتِلْكَ الْأَمْثَالُ نَضْرِبُهَا لِلنَّاسِ لَعَلَّهُمْ يَتَفَكَّرُونَ

{And We present these examples for mankind perchance they would reflect.} Sūrah al-Ḥashr

And He, the All Mighty, stated,

مَثَلُ الَّذِينَ يُنْفِقُونَ أَمْوَالَهُمْ فِي سَبِيلِ اللَّهِ كَمَثَلِ حَبَّةٍ أَنْبَتَتْ سَبْعَ سَنَابِلَ فِي كُلِّ سُنْبُلَةٍ مِائَةُ حَبَّةٍ وَاللَّهُ يُضَاعِفُ لِمَنْ يَشَاءُ وَاللَّهُ وَاسِعٌ عَلِيمٌ

{The example of those who spend their wealth in the cause of Allāh is that of a grain that sprouts into seven ears, each bearing one hundred grains. And Allāh multiplies (the reward even more) to whoever He wills. For Allāh is All-Bountiful, All-Knowing.} Sūrah al-Baqarah: 261

In an effort to benefit the Muslim community, we have extracted sections of the book in which the author skillfully presents over 20 parables that illustrate the severe dangers of worldly life. We sincerely hope that readers find great benefit in these parables and deeply reflect on their meanings, enabling them to be cautious of these harms, just as the great scholar of Islām Imām an-Nawawī mentioned in lines of poetry in the introduction to his renowned book *Riyādh as-Sālihīn,*

إِنَّ للَّهِ عِبَادًا فُطَنَا ... طَلَّقُوا الدُّنْيَا وخَافُوا الفِتَنَا

نَظَرُوا فيهَا فَلَمَّا عَلِمُوا ... أَنَّهَا لَيْسَتْ لِحَيٍّ وَطَنَا

جَعَلُوها لُجَّةً واتَّخَذُوا ... صَالِحَ الأَعمالِ فيها سُفُنا

Indeed, Allāh has intelligent servants.

They have forsaken the world out of fear of its calamities.

They looked at it and when they realized it is not a permanent abode for a person who desires true life.

Hence, they made it (the world) an ocean, and they made righteous deeds the boat (which they use to cross it). [6]

Islamic Reminders Publications

Newark, New Jersey

United States of America

6 These lines were also attributed to the great scholar of Islām Imām ash-Shāf'ī.

Imām Ibn al-Qayyim mentioned about the life of this world,[7]

1. The closest (example) thing to this world is like a person experiencing a dream in which he sees what he loves and what he hates. Once he awakes, he realizes it was not a reality.

2. Another example of it is like an old woman ugly in her appearance and demeanor, and extremely treacherous to her husbands. She adorns herself with every type of adornment for suitors and covers all her flaws. Those whose sight did not go beyond her outward appearance were deceived by her and when they sought marriage, she said,

"There is no dowry except the exchange of the Hereafter. We (I and the Hereafter) are co-wives, and our union is neither permitted nor lawful."

Thus, the suitors preferred what was immediate, and they said,

"There is no harm in uniting with the one you love."

When her mask was removed and her belt was untied,[8] every calamity and misfortune was revealed. Among them, are those who immediately divorced her and were relieved, while others chose to stay, and their wedding night was filled with wailing and crying.

---

7 The numbering of these parables was created by the publisher for clarity. (P.N.)

8 Indicating that the person has deeply indulged in her (i.e., the Dunyā). (T.N.)

By Allāh, indeed her caller has made the call to all of creation, saying,

'Come to no success!'

Those who are diligent and devote to her continued their pursuit for her from morning to evening. They (even) travelled through the night, but in the morning, they were saddened that their journey was of no benefit. They continued in search of her, but no one returned except with broken limbs. They fell into her net and surrendered to destruction."[9]

3. The servant of Allāh has three states:

- A state in which he was nothing, which is before his existence.
- Another state from the moment of his death until his eternal abode, whether in Paradise or in Hell. Then, his soul returns to his body, and he is recompensed for his deeds, and he dwells in one of the two abodes in eternal bliss.
- Between these two states, which is after his existence and before his death, there is a moderate state, which is the days of his life.

If one considers the amount of time in this state and compares it to the other two states, he will realize that it is less than the blink of an eye in the span of worldly life. Whoever views the world with this perspective will not incline towards it or care about how

9 These two parables were mentioned by the author on pgs. 436 – 437. The numbers for the following parables have been adjusted to include the first two parables previously mentioned. (P.N.)

his days are spent in it, whether in distress and hardship, or in ease and luxury. That is why the Messenger of Allāh (ﷺ) did not put one brick upon another nor construct buildings,[10] rather, he said,

مَالي وللدُّنيا إنما مَثَلي ومَثَلُ الدُّنيا كراكِبٍ قالَ في ظلٍّ شَجرةٍ ثم راحَ وتركَها

"What have I to do with the world? The example of me and the world is like that of a rider who rests in the shade of a tree, then goes and leaves it."[11]

He (ﷺ) also said,

ما الدُّنْيا في الآخِرةِ إلاّ مِثلُ ما يُجْعَلُ أحَدُكمْ إصبعَه في اليمِّ ، فلْيَنْظُر بِمَ يَرْجعُ

"The world in the Hereafter is like one of you dipping his finger in the sea; let him see what he brings back."[12]

This was also indicated by Jesus (عَلَيْهِ ٱلسَّلَامُ) when he said,

"The world is a bridge, so cross it, but do not build on it."

This is a valid analogy, for life is a passage to the Hereafter. The cradle is the first pillar at the beginning of the bridge, and the grave is the second pillar at its end. Some people have crossed half of the bridge, others have crossed two-thirds, and some have only one step left, unaware of it. Regardless, crossing is inevitable.

---

10 What's apparent is that the author intends that the Prophet (ﷺ) did not construct lofty buildings in this life. (T.N.)

11 Reported in *at-Tirmidhī* (2377), *Ibn Mājah* (4109), and declared authentic by Shaykh al-Albānī in *Ṣaḥīḥ at-Tirmidhī*

12 Reported in *Muslim* (2858)

Therefore, whoever stops on the bridge and begins to build on it and adorn it with various decorations, while rushing to cross, is indeed extremely ignorant and foolish. [13]

4. The desires of the world in the heart are like the desires of food in the stomach. The servant will find, at the time of death, regarding the desires of the world in his heart, a feeling of disgust, aversion, and ugliness similar to what he experiences from delicious foods when their purpose is fulfilled in the stomach. Just as the more delicious and fattier the food is, the more repulsive its feces is, so too is every desire in the soul. The more delightful and stronger it is, the more painful it will be to abandon it at the time of death, just as a person is distressed by the loss of his beloved when he is separated from them, proportional to his love for the beloved.

It is reported in the *Musnad*, that the Prophet (صَلَّى ٱللَّهُ عَلَيْهِ وَسَلَّمَ) said to Dhakwān ibn Safyān,

"Do you not eat your food when it is prepared and salted, and then you drink water and milk?"

He said, "Yes."

The Prophet (صَلَّى ٱللَّهُ عَلَيْهِ وَسَلَّمَ) said, "Where does it end up?"

He said, "In what is known."

The Prophet (صَلَّى ٱللَّهُ عَلَيْهِ وَسَلَّمَ) said, "Indeed, Allāh, the Almighty, has struck a similitude for the world based on where the food of the

13 This parable, and those that follow were mentioned by the author from pgs. 444 – 475

son of Ādam ends up." [14]

Some of the Salaf used to say to their companions,

"Come, and I will show you the world."

They would take them to a garbage dump and say,

"Look at their fruits, their chickens, their honey, and their fat."

5. Another example of this world and its people who are preoccupied with their pleasure, neglecting the Hereafter and its consequences, are like people who boarded a ship that took them to an island. The captain ordered them to disembark to fulfill their needs but warned them about delaying and fearing the ship's departure. They scattered across the island. Some fulfilled their needs and hurried back to the ship, finding empty space (onboard). They took the widest and most comfortable places, best suited to their desires.

Some stood on the island, admiring its amazing flowers, its wonderful lights, listening to the birds' melodies, and admiring the beauty of its stones. Then he reminded himself of missing the ship and its swift passage, and the danger of its departure. He returned and found only a narrow place, so he sat there.

Another individual burdened himself by carrying beautiful stones and extraordinary flowers. When he returned to the ship, he found only a very restricted place, adding to his burden and discomfort. He could not throw it (the stones and flowers) away, nor did he find a place for it on the ship. Consequently, he carried

14 Reported in the *Musnad* of Imām Aḥmad vol. 3, pg. 452

it on his shoulders and regretted taking it, although his regret was of no avail. Eventually, the flowers withered, and their fragrance turned unpleasant, causing him great discomfort due to the foul odor.

Others entered into the dense foliage (of the island), forgetting the ship, and wandering further in their leisure. Even when the captain called out to the people upon departure, his voice didn't reach them because they were engrossed in their amusements. Sometimes they ate fruits, smelled flowers, or admired the beauty of the trees, all the while afraid of being attacked by a wild animal. They were afraid that thorns might prick their clothes or feet, a branch might wound them, or pierce their garments and expose their bodies, or a loud noise might startle them.

Some managed to catch the ship before it departed, but found no space left on it, so they died on the shore.

Some of them were preoccupied with their amusements, so they were devoured by wild animals or bitten by snakes.

Others were lost until they fell on their faces and perished.

This is an example of the people of this world, preoccupied with their immediate fortunes, forgetting their origin and the consequences of their actions. How ugly it is for a rational person to be deceived by stones and plants that turn to dust, occupying his mind and hindering his salvation, but not accompanying him (in the Hereafter).

6. The enticement of people by worldly life and their weak faith in the Hereafter

Ibn Abī Dunyā said that Isḥāq bin Ismā'īl narrated to us, who narrated from Rūḥ bin 'Ubāda, who narrated from Hishām bin Ḥassān, who narrated from al-Ḥasan, who said,

"It reached me that the Messenger of Allāh (صَلَّى ٱللَّهُ عَلَيْهِ وَسَلَّمَ) said to his companions,

'My example, your example, and the example of the world are like a group of people who embarked on a journey through a desert. They reached a point where they could not discern whether they consumed more provisions or what remained, so they depleted their supplies, exhausted their water, and remained in the middle of the desert with no provisions or supplies left. At that point, they realized their imminent destruction. While they were in such a state, a man appeared before them, well-groomed. They said (to themselves),

'For sure he has recently arrived.'

When he reached them, he said, 'What is your condition?'

They said, 'As you can see.'

He then said, 'What if I were to guide you to water and green pastures, what would you give me (in return)?'

They said, 'We would never disobey you in the least.'

He then guided them to water and green pastures. They remained there for as long as Allāh willed, then the man returned and said, 'O people, prepare to depart.'

They said, 'To where?'

He said, 'To (an area that has) water that is unlike (better than) this water, and green pastures that are unlike (better than) these green pastures.'

Upon hearing this, most of the people responded, 'By Allāh, we did not expect to find this, and what would we do with something better?'

The rest, who were the smaller number, said (to the others), 'Did you not give this man your promises and agreements with Allāh not to disobey him in anything, and he proved truthful in his initial words? By Allāh, he will prove truthful in his final words.'

So, those who followed him departed with him, while the rest stayed behind. Their enemies came upon them, and they were taken as captives or killed.'"[15]

7. The Prophet (صَلَّى ٱللَّهُ عَلَيْهِ وَسَلَّمَ) likened this world and its people to the shade of a tree, where a traveler seeks shelter under it on a hot day, then departs and leaves it behind.[16]

Reflect upon the beauty of this analogy and its resemblance to reality. Just like the shade of a tree, this world is green and fleeting, disappearing gradually like the shade. The servant is a traveler on his way to his Lord, and when a traveler sees a tree on a hot day, it is not befitting for him to build a permanent dwelling under it or make it his final destination. Rather, he seeks shelter under it as needed, and when that need is fulfilled, he continues his journey, leaving it behind.

15 *Dham ad-Dunyā* and *az-Zuhd* by Ibn Mubārak
16 This ḥadīth was previously mentioned in footnote #10.

8. It (the life of this world) is likened to dipping one's finger into the sea, and what remains on the finger from the sea represents this world, in relation to the Hereafter.[17]

This analogy is also among the best examples. For this world is temporary and finite, even if its duration were longer than it actually is, while the Hereafter is eternal with no end or interruption. That which has a limited duration can never be compared to what is endless.

If we were to assume that the heavens and the Earth were filled with mustard seeds, and every thousand years a bird took a mustard seed and flew away, the mustard seeds would end, but the Hereafter would remain eternally.

The ratio of this world in comparison to the Hereafter is like the ratio of one mustard seed to a bundle of mustard seeds. Therefore, if the sea was made ink and refilled seven times to write the Words of Allāh, and the trees of the Earth were pens, the sea and pens would be exhausted, and the Words of Allāh would remain. Indeed, His words have no beginning or end, while the sea and the pens are finite."[18]

Imām Aḥmad and others have said, "Allāh has always been speaking when He wills."[19]

---

17 This ḥadīth was previously mentioned in footnote #11.

18 Allāh, the Most High, said in Sūrah Luqmān verse 27,

وَلَوْ أَنَّمَا فِي الْأَرْضِ مِن شَجَرَةٍ أَقْلَامٌ وَالْبَحْرُ يَمُدُّهُ مِن بَعْدِهِ سَبْعَةُ أَبْحُرٍ مَّا نَفِدَتْ كَلِمَاتُ اللَّهِ ۗ إِنَّ اللَّهَ عَزِيزٌ حَكِيمٌ

{If all the trees on earth were pens and the ocean (were ink), refilled by seven other oceans, the Words of Allāh would not be exhausted. Surely Allāh is Almighty, All-Wise.}

19 The statement of Imām Aḥmad is present in his book titled *ar-Rad 'ala az-Zanadiqah wal Jahmiyah.*

His perfection necessitates His speech. His perfection is inherent, so He is complete, and the speaker is more perfect than the non-speaker. He, the Exalted, does not experience fatigue or weariness from speaking. He creates and manages His creation with His words. His words are what brought His creation and commands into existence. This is the reality of His sovereignty, lordship, and divinity. He is indeed a Lord, a King, a God. There is no deity worthy of worship but Him.

The intended meaning (of this parable) is that this world is just a breath in the vastness of the Hereafter, a mere moment in its eternity.

9. The Prophet (ﷺ) likened this world in a ḥadīth reported in *Ṣaḥiḥ al-Bukhārī* and *Ṣaḥiḥ Muslim* on the authority of by Abū Sa'īd al-Khudrī - may Allāh be pleased with him - who said,

"The Messenger of Allāh (ﷺ) stood and addressed the people, saying,

'By Allāh, what I fear most for you is what Allāh will bring forth for you from the pleasures of this world.'

Upon hearing this, a man said, 'O Messenger of Allāh, can good bring forth evil?'

The Messenger of Allāh (ﷺ) remained silent, then he said,

'What did you say?'

The man said,

'O Messenger of Allāh, can good bring forth evil?'

The Messenger of Allāh (صَلَّى ٱللَّهُ عَلَيْهِ وَسَلَّمَ) replied,

'Indeed, good can only come from good. However, from what grows in the spring, some of it destroys (animals) because of overeating, or brings them close to death. On the other hand, there are animals that eat green crops and when their bellies are full, they face the sun, defecate, and urinate, and then return to graze. Blessed is the one who takes wealth rightfully. However, the one who takes wealth unlawfully is like the one who eats without being satisfied.'"[20]

The Prophet (صَلَّى ٱللَّهُ عَلَيْهِ وَسَلَّمَ) clarified that what he fears for them is the worldly life. He called it a flower and likened it to its pleasant fragrance, beautiful appearance, and temporary nature, but indicated that what comes after it is better and everlasting. When he mentioned that some of what grows in the spring can cause death due to overeating, or brings them (animals) close to death, this is one of the best analogies warning against becoming engrossed in worldly affairs. Just as grazing animals enjoy the spring grass, but they may perish as a result of overeating.

'*Habatan*' refers to the swelling of an animal's belly from excessive feeding or illness. It is said that a man or animal experienced *habat*, if they are afflicted with this illness.

When Hārith ibn Māzin ibn 'Amr ibn Tamīm experienced this during his journey and died due to overeating, it was attributed to '*al-habata*'.

Similarly, the greed for wealth is fatal, as one's greed and eagerness for it can destroy him. If it doesn't destroy him, it's likely to bring him close to death, as indicated by the phrase "*aw yalim*" (or become afflicted). Many wealthy individuals have been killed by their own wealth because they were greedy in accumulating

20 Reported by a*l-Bukhārī* (6427) and *Muslim* (1052)

it, and others needed it but couldn't reach it except by killing those who possessed the wealth, or similar to killing them, such as harming or oppressing them.

The phrase *"except what eats green crops"* is a representation of someone who takes from the world what they need, like a sheep eating grass according to its needs. It eats until its belly is full or, in another version, its sides extend due to its fullness from food. The sides here refer to the flanks of the animal, which are the sides of its belly.

The phrase *"faced the sun, defecated and urinated"* has three benefits:

First: It indicates that after taking what it needed from the pasture, it left it and its subsequent exposure to the sun's warmth allowed what it ate to be digested.

Second: It turned away from what could harm it, such as the greed in the pasture, and turned towards what could benefit it by facing the sun, which aids in the digestion of what it consumed.[21]

Third: It expelled what it gathered from the pasture in its stomach through urination and defecation, thereby relieving itself.

If it remained in the stomach, it would kill the animal, just as grazing animals might die if they retain urine and feces in their stomachs. Similarly, the one who gathers wealth must do as this

---

21 It's truly extraordinary how some of the great scholars of Islām, such as Imām Ibn al-Qayyim, not only possessed knowledge of Islām, but they also possessed extensive knowledge regarding science and medicine. The information mentioned here by the author was recently discovered by medical experts who informed that exposure to sunlight, which is the best source of vitamin D, aids in digestion and promotes good stomach health. (T.N.)

sheep did.[22]

The beginning of the ḥadīth, "the example of greed in accumulating worldly goods," refers to someone who is eager to gather wealth. Their example is like the animal that is led by its greed for food, which ultimately leads to its death due to overeating or illness. Thus, the one who is greedy and eager for wealth is either doomed or near destruction. This is evidenced by the fact that spring brings forth various types of edible seeds and herbs, which animals continue to eat until their stomachs swell beyond their capacity, causing their intestines to burst and them to perish. Likewise, the one who accumulates wealth unlawfully or misuses it, will be harmed by hoarding it.

The last part of the ḥadīth is an analogy of the moderate person who takes from the world what they need, just as the sheep benefited from its grazing, without being led by greed or eagerness to take more than necessary. This person takes what he needs, then does what benefits him with it. The analogy of the animal's urination and excretion is an example of the person who extracts his money rightfully where its confinement and retention would harm him. Thus, he avoids harm by taking only what he needs and prevents further harm by not holding onto it, much like an animal avoids destruction by urinating and excreting.

In this narration, there is an indication of moderation and balance between excess in grazing, which is harmful due to its abundance, and refraining from it entirely, leading to starvation. The narration also advises those who possess abundant wealth to preserve their sustenance and health in their bodies and hearts by spending it, rather than hoarding it, as hoarding harms them, and success is from Allāh.

---

22 i.e., Taking what is needed, benefiting from it, and avoiding harm by spending it where it is necessary, which is similar to the sheep's act of relieving itself. (T.N.)

10. Amr ibn Shu'ayb narrated from his father, who narrated from Sulaimān ibn Yasār, who narrated from Maymūna who said: "The Messenger of Allāh (صَلَّىٰاللَّهُعَلَيْهِوَسَلَّمَ) said to 'Amr ibn al-'Ās,

إِنَّ الدُّنْيَا حُلْوَةٌ خَضِرَةٌ، فَمَنِ اتَّقَى فِيهَا وَأَصْلَحَ، وَإِلا فَهُوَ كَالآكِلِ وَلا يَشْبَع، فَبُعْدُ النَّاسِ كَبُعْدِ الْكَوْكَبَيْنِ: أَحَدُهُمَا يَطْلُعُ مِنَ المشْرِقِ، وَالآخَرُ يَغِيبُ بِالمغْرِبِ

'The world is sweet and green. Whoever fears Allāh in it and rectifies his affairs (will be successful), and if not, then he will be like someone who eats and is never satisfied. The difference between them is like the distance between two stars: one appears in the east, while the other sets in the west."

The Prophet (صَلَّىٰاللَّهُعَلَيْهِوَسَلَّمَ) highlighted its lushness to inform how eyes are captivated by the world, and he highlighted its sweetness to reveal the hearts' desires, and the allure of its lushness and sweetness to its inhabitants, especially since they are created from it and in it.

As one said,

"We are the children of the earth, and from it we grow... And whatever you come from is always loved by you."

The people are divided into two groups regarding it:

- One is righteous and God-fearing, so their righteousness and rectitude prevent them from being engrossed in it, indulging in its pleasures, taking it unlawfully, or misappropriating it.

- If one does not fear Allāh and rectify his affairs, his

> desires, strength, and eagerness will be directed towards acquiring it, and he will be like someone who eats without ever being satisfied.

This is one of the best analogies because the intended purpose of eating is to preserve health and strength, which are contingent upon necessity, not the act itself. Whoever prioritizes their desires over their intended purpose will never be satisfied. That's why Imām Aḥmad said,

"The world's little will suffice, but its abundance will not."[23]

He indicated the disparity among people in terms of their level of righteousness and rectitude, versus indulgence in worldly pleasures and desires.

The analogy of two stars, one rising and the other setting, illustrates the disparity between two individuals in terms of their righteousness and rectitude. Their levels vary, just as the positions of stars differ in the sky.

11. It reported on the authority of Mustawrid ibn Shaddād who stated,

"I was with a group of people who stood with the Messenger of Allāh (ﷺ) near a dead sheep, when the Messenger of Allāh (ﷺ) said,

'Do you think this is insignificant to its owners until they disposed of it?'

They said, 'They threw it away because it is insignificant, O Messenger of Allāh'

23 *Ṭabaqāt al-Ḥanābilah* vol.1, pg. 10

He said, 'By the One in Whose hand is the soul of Muḥammad, the world is more insignificant to Allāh than this (sheep) is to its owners.' at-Tirmidhī classified this ḥadīth as Ḥasan Ṣaḥiḥ.[24]

He did not limit its comparison to the dead sheep; rather, he made it clear that it is less significant to Allāh than it is.

In Imām Aḥmad's *Musnad*, the wording of this ḥadīth reads:

"By the One in Whose hand is my soul, the world is more insignificant to Allāh than this dead sheep is to its owners."[25]

He emphasized this statement with an oath. So, if something like that is more insignificant and despicable to Allāh than a dead sheep is to its owners, then the love and affection for it is less significant to Allāh than that dead sheep. And the fact that it is a young dead sheep, is even less significant to them than it being a full-grown sheep, because they might benefit from its wool or tan its skin. As for the young dead sheep, it is utterly insignificant. And Allāh is the One sought for help.

12. The world is likened to an ocean that all of creation must cross in order to reach the shore, where their homes, settlements, and destinations lie. It cannot be crossed except with the ship of salvation, which Allāh sent His messengers to inform the nations about and to order them to build them and board them. This ship symbolizes obedience to Allāh, obedience to His messengers, worship of Him alone, and sincere actions for Him, longing for the Hereafter, and striving for it.

---

24 Good and acceptable

25 Reported in at-*Tirmidhī* (2321), *Ibn Mājah* (4111), and the *Musnad* of Aḥmad (18021)

Those who are successful rise and board the ship, abstaining from plunging into the sea when they realize that diving into it or swimming across it is not possible.

The foolish ones however, find it difficult to build the ship, operate its machinery, and board it. They decided to plunge into the sea, thinking that they can swim if they fail (to float). They are the majority of the people of this world. They plunged into it, and when they fail to float, they tried to swim until they drowned. Those who boarded the ship are saved, just as Noah's companions were saved, while (the rest of) the people of the Earth drowned.

Consider this analogy, and you will see how it aligns with reality.

13. This world is like a jar filled with honey. Flies discover it and approach it. Some of them settled on the edge of the jar and began to consume the honey until they were satisfied, then they flew away.

Others, driven by greed, threw themselves into the midst of the honey. Their immersion in it didn't give them the opportunity to enjoy it for long before they drowned in the middle of the honey.

14. The example of seeds scattered on the ground, with each seed placed in a trap. Around these seeds, there are traps, while some areas are trap-free. Then birds approach. Some birds are content with what's on the sides, and don't risk entering the traps. They take what they need and then depart. Others, driven by greed, invade most of the seeds. They don't stop eating until they cry due to being captured in the traps.

15. This is the example of a man who lights a large fire, attracting moths and grasshoppers with its light, thus, they plunge into it. Some insects are aware of the danger, so they stay away and use the fire for light and warmth from a distance.

The Prophet (ﷺ) referred to this in a ḥadīth narrated by Mālik ibn Ismā'īl, who narrated from Ḥafs ibn Ḥamīd, from Ikrimah, on the authority of Ibn 'Abbās who said that 'Umar said that the Prophet (ﷺ) said,

"I am holding onto your waist ties from falling into the fire, and you are overpowering me and rushing towards it."

In another narration he said,

إنَّما مَثَلِي ومَثَلُ النَّاسِ كَمَثَلِ رَجُلٍ اسْتَوْقَدَ نارًا، فَلَمَّا أضاءَتْ ما حَوْلَهُ جَعَلَ الفَراشُ وهذِه الدَّوابُّ الَّتي تَقَعُ في النَّارِ يَقَعْنَ فيها، فَجَعَلَ يَنْزِعُهُنَّ ويَغْلِبْنَهُ فَيَقْتَحِمْنَ فيها، فأنا آخُذُ بحُجَزِكُمْ عَنِ النَّارِ، وهُمْ يَقْتَحِمُونَ فيها

"My example and yours are like a man who kindles a fire, and when it has lit, the bugs and rodents flock to it. I am holding onto your waist ties from falling into the fire, but you are overpowering me and are rushing towards it."[26]

This analogy applies to those immersed in worldly matters. The messengers call them to the Hereafter, but they are preoccupied with the world, just like bugs (rushing towards fire).

---

26 Reported by *al-Bukhārī* (6483) and *Muslim* (2284)

16. A group of people embarked on a journey with their wealth and families. They passed by a valley with an abundance of water and fruits, so they settled there, pitched their tents, and built their homes and palaces. Then a man known to them for his sincerity, honesty, and trustworthy nature passed by them and said,

"I have seen with my own eyes an army behind this valley, heading towards you. Follow me, and I will lead you away from the enemy's path, and you will be safe."

A small group obeyed him, but he shouted, "O people, salvation, salvation! You are going to be attacked, you are going to be attacked!"

Those who heard him rushed to gather their families and belongings and follow him. However, some hesitated, saying,

"How can we leave this valley, where we have our livestock, wealth, and homes that we have settled in?"

The sincere advisor told them, "Each of you should take with him what he can carry of his belongings, or else you will be taken captive, and your wealth will be plundered."

The leaders of the people, attached to their wealth and properties, found it difficult to leave and abandon the luxuries they were enjoying. They hesitated to leave what they considered their pleasure and comfort. Each foolish person said,

"I should follow those who stayed behind. They have more wealth and belongings than me, so whatever happens to them will happen to me with them."

Meanwhile, the few who followed the wise advisor found salvation, while the army attacked and looted the people who remained in the valley.

The Prophet (ﷺ) mentioned this same analogy in the ḥadīth reported in *Ṣaḥiḥ al-Bukhārī* and *Ṣaḥiḥ Muslim* on the authority of Abū Burda, who narrated on the authority of Abū Mūsá, who said that the Prophet (ﷺ) said,

إِنَّمَا مَثَلِي وَمَثَلُ مَا بَعَثَنِي اللَّهُ بِهِ كَمَثَلِ رَجُلٍ أَتَى قَوْمًا فَقَالَ يَا قَوْمِ إِنِّي رَأَيْتُ الْجَيْشَ بِعَيْنِي وَإِنِّي أَنَا النَّذِيرُ الْعُرْيَانُ فَالنَّجَاءَ النَّجَاءَ فَأَطَاعَهُ طَائِفَةٌ مِنْ قَوْمِهِ فَأَدْلَجُوا فَانْطَلَقُوا عَلَى مَهْلِهِمْ فَنَجَوْا وَكَذَّبَتْ طَائِفَةٌ مِنْهُمْ فَأَصْبَحُوا مَكَانَهُمْ فَصَبَّحَهُمُ الْجَيْشُ فَأَهْلَكَهُمْ وَاجْتَاحَهُمْ فَذَلِكَ مَثَلُ مَنْ أَطَاعَنِي فَاتَّبَعَ مَا جِئْتُ بِهِ وَمثل من عَصَانِي وَكذب بِمَا جِئْتُ بِهِ مِنَ الْحَقِّ

"My example and the example of what Allāh has sent me with is like a man who came to his people and said, 'O people, indeed I am a clear warner to you. I have seen the army with my own eyes. The only means of escape is to escape itself.' A group from among his people obeyed him and left quietly at night, and they were saved. But another group from among them disbelieved him and stayed in their place. When the army came upon them, it destroyed and overpowered them. This is the example of those who obey me and follow what I have brought, and the example of those who disobey me and reject the truth I have brought."[27]

27 Reported by *al-Bukhārī* (2283) and *Muslim* (7283)

17. A man prepared a house, decorated it, and furnished it with all kinds of amenities, then invited people to it. Whenever someone entered, he would seat them on a luxurious couch, serve them delicious food on golden plates, and offer them all they desired. He also ordered his servants and slaves to attend to their every need. The wise person recognized that all of this was the host's property and possessions. He enjoyed the amenities and hospitality during his stay in the house without becoming attached to them. He relied on the host for everything, just as a guest does, sitting where he was seated and eating what was served without asking for more. He was content with the host's generosity and did not inquire beyond that, trusting the host's knowledge and generosity with his guests.

On the other hand, the fool became attached to the house's comfort and amenities, considering them his own possession. He rearranged the furniture according to his desires and moved the amenities to a hidden place in the house to claim ownership over them. Whenever the host brought something new, he considered it his own and separated himself from the other guests. Eventually, when the owner of the house discovered his actions, he expelled him violently, confiscating everything he had taken, leaving him with nothing. This resulted in the fool's disgrace and humiliation in front of the host, his servants, and guests.

Reflecting on this example reveals its profound truth. As Abdullāh ibn Mas'ūd – may Allāh be pleased with him - said,

"Everyone in this world is a guest, and he has a departure. The guest enjoys what is offered, but the departure is imminent."

Additionally, it is reported in *Ṣaḥiḥ al-Bukhārī* and *Ṣaḥiḥ Muslim* on the authority of Anas ibn Mālik, who said,

"A son of Abū Talḥa from Umm Sulaim died, so she said to her family, 'Do not inform Abū Talḥa until I inform him myself.' She then prepared dinner for him. When he had eaten and drunk, she beautified herself more than she used to before. He had intercourse with her, and when she felt that he was satisfied she said, 'O Abū Talḥa, if some people loaned something to a family, and then requested it back, is it appropriate for the family to refuse to return it?'[28] He said, 'No'. She said, 'Then seek the reward (from Allāh) for the death of your son.' He became upset and said, 'You have left me uninformed until we had intercourse, and then you inform me of the death of my son?' He then approached the Prophet (صَلَّى ٱللَّهُ عَلَيْهِ وَسَلَّمَ) and informed him of what occurred. The Prophet (صَلَّى ٱللَّهُ عَلَيْهِ وَسَلَّمَ) supplicated saying, 'May Allāh bless your night.'"[29]

18. A group of people traveled through a desert and unexpectedly faced severe thirst. They reached the sea, but its water was bitter and salty. Because of their extreme thirst, they did not perceive its bitterness and saltiness when they drank from it. Instead, they found themselves becoming even thirstier with each sip until their stomachs were ruptured, and they died of thirst. The wise among them understood that the sea was saline, and the more they drank from it, the thirstier they'd become. They distanced themselves from it until they found fertile land. They dug a well and found fresh, sweet water gushing from it. They drank, quenched their thirst, and called out to their brothers who were still at the edge

28 This is the point of the ḥadīth that the author intends to extract an example from. Everything in this life belongs to Allāh, and He will eventually take it back (i.e., at the time of death). (T.N.)

29 Reported by *al-Bukhārī* (1301) and *Muslim* (2144)

of the sea, inviting them to the fresh water. Some mocked them, some turned away satisfied with what they had, while others responded one after another. This example was also mentioned by Jesus (عَلَيْهِ ٱلسَّلَامُ), who said,

"The seeker of the world is like one who drinks from the sea; the more he drinks, the more thirsty he becomes until it kills him."[30]

19. A man had three brothers, and he had to embark on a long journey. He called his brothers and said,

"You see what is needed for this long journey, and I am in great need of your help now."

One of them said, "I was your brother up to this point, but from now on, I am no longer your brother or companion, and I have nothing to offer."

The second brother said, "I have been your brother and companion until now, and I am with you until I prepare you for your journey and help you board your ride. But from there on, I am not your companion."

The traveler replied, "I need your company on my journey," to which the brother responded, "There is no way for you to have that."

The traveler then said, "You have not benefited me at all."

Finally, he asked the third brother, "What do you have?"

The third brother replied, "I was your companion in your health and sickness, and I am your companion now. I will accompany

30 *Dham ad-Dunyā* (342)

you on your journey, ride with you, stay with you wherever you go, and never leave you. When you reach your destination, I will still be your companion there. I will never leave you."

The traveler realized the true worth of his brothers and wished that he had preferred the third one over the other two.

The first brother represents his wealth, the second represents his relatives and family, while the third represents one's deeds.

This example is narrated in a ḥadīth, although its chain of narration is not authentic. It is mentioned by Abū Ja'far al-Uqīlī in his book ad-Du'af'ā narrated by Ibn Shihāb, on the authority of 'Urwah, who narrated on the authority of 'Āisha. It's also reported on the authority of Ibn Musayib, who reported on the authority of 'Āisha, who attributed the statement to the Prophet (صَلَّىٰ ٱللَّهُ عَلَيْهِ وَسَلَّمَ). It is an accurate parable, in alignment with reality.

20. This is one of the best examples. A king built a palace that eyes had never seen, and ears had never heard, and more spacious and finer for the pleasures of the soul than one could ever imagine. He then built a road leading to it and sent a caller inviting people to it. He stationed a beautiful woman on the road adorned with all kinds of ornaments and jewelry. People passed by her, and he assigned assistants and servants to her. He placed a large amount of provisions with her and gave her and servants autonomy to give to travelers on the road to the king's palace. He then instructed her and her assistants saying,

"Whoever passes and doesn't look at you and is not distracted by you from me, and he only wants provisions to reach me, then serve him, give him provisions, and do not prevent him from his journey to me. Rather, assist him with everything he needs in his journey.

But whoever extends his eyes towards you, finds satisfaction in you, prioritizes you over me, and seeks your companionship, then give him a severe punishment and make him suffer the ultimate humiliation. Exploit him and make him run after you like a wild beast. Likewise, whoever consumes from you, deceive him for a while, then retrieve everything from him and strip him of it entirely. Command your followers and slaves over him, and whenever someone exceeds in their love, reverence, and honor for you, meet them with the likes of disdain, humiliation, and abandonment until their souls are shattered for you in regret."

Reflect upon this analogy and what is mentioned of worldly affairs, compared to what is mentioned about the Hereafter. Allāh is the One sought for help.

This analogy is taken from the tradition narrated from Allāh, the Almighty,

"O world, serve one who served Me and enslave the one who served you."[31]

21. A king built a city in the best of places, its air was refreshing and its waters abundant. He dug its rivers and planted its trees, then said to his subjects,

"Race to the best places in it, for whoever reaches a place first, it shall be his. But whoever remains behind, others will beat him to it."

31 Reported by al-Khatīb al-Baghdādī in *Tārikh Baghdād*, and he declared it to be fabricated. (T.N.)

Those who lagged behind found that others had taken their homes and occupied their dwellings in the city, so they were left with regret and disappointment.

The king then erected a racecourse and planted a large tree in it, providing extended shade with flowing water underneath and all kinds of fruits on its branches, with amazing birds singing in its shade.

He warned the people saying,

"Do not be deceived by this tree and its shade, for it will soon be uprooted. Its shade will vanish, its fruits will cease, and its birds will die.

As for the city of the king, its sustenance is perpetual, its shade enduring, and its bliss eternal. In it are treasures beyond what eyes have seen, ears have heard, or hearts have ever imagined."

The people heard about the city and rushed in search of it, their faces bright with anticipation. On their way, they passed by the tree after a journey filled with exhaustion, hardships, and thirst. When they all gathered under its shade, they enjoyed its coolness, tasted its fruits, and listened to the chirping of its birds. They were told,

"You have gathered here to protect yourselves (from the sun) and gather your provisions before the race. Prepare yourselves, for when the signal is given, you must compete."

But the majority exclaimed,

"How can we leave this cool shade, flowing water, ripe fruits, comfort, and rest to enter into heat, dust, exhaustion, a long journey, and dry throats that destroy our stomachs? How can we trade the present joy for a distant unseen future, and abandon what we have for what we don't have? A grain that one has in his hand today is far better than a promised grain tomorrow. Take what you see, and leave what you have heard. We are the people of today, and this is a present life. How can we leave it for a distant life in a land we do not know when we will reach?"

One person from each thousand[32] (who understood the reality) stood up and said,

"By Allāh, we will not remain under this fleeting shade of a tree that will soon be uprooted, lose its shade, and its birds will soon die.

We will not abandon the race for the sake of this fleeting shade, when there is an eternal shade and everlasting bliss awaiting us. This (deciding to remain here) could only be done by the most foolish of fools.

Is it befitting for the traveler, when taking rest under the shade, to put his tent there and make it his place of residence, fearing harm from heat and cold? Is this anything but folly? This is a true race and one must be prompt.

The verdict of death in the wilderness is pending,
this world is but a temporary abode.
Pursue your aims swiftly, for indeed
your lives are but a journey among journeys.
Race forth and hasten like racing horses,
to regain, for they are but fleeting moments.
Avoid dwelling under passing shade,

32 One person from each thousand indicates that a very small number of people truly understood the reality of the situation, and preferred to continue the journey, instead of remaining under the tree. (T.N.)

for you are on a journey in this world.

Whoever hopes for a good life in it,

is building hopes on the brink of ruin.

True life, real life, after its departure,

is in the abode of those who precede, the most honorable abode."

The fortunate ones rushed into the race without being bothered by the scarcity of companions, and they marched with determination, unaffected by the criticism of those who criticized them in their journey.

Meanwhile, those who remained behind slept under the tree's shade. By Allāh, it wasn't long before the tree's branches withered, its leaves fell, its fruits ceased to grow, its flowing water stopped, and it was uprooted from its base.

The people found themselves exposed to scorching heat, regretting the livelihood they had abandoned under the tree's shade. The once-cooling shade turned into a blazing fire, surrounding those underneath it. None of them could escape, and they cried out,

"Where are those who shared the shade with us but left us?

It was said to them, "Raise your sight and look at them in their mansions."

They saw them from far in mansions in the city of the king, where they enjoyed all kinds of pleasures. Their regret intensified when they saw them, and their disappointment increased as barriers prevented them from reaching what they desired.

وَمَا ظَلَمْنَاهُمْ وَلَٰكِن كَانُوا هُمُ الظَّالِمِينَ

{We wronged them not, but they wronged

themselves.} Sūrah az-Zukhruf: 76

22. The Prophet (ﷺ) gave a simile about the world like a garment that is torn from end to end, with only a thread remaining at its edge.

Ibn Abī Dunyā narrated from Fudayl ibn Ja'far, who narrated from Wahb ibn Ḥammād, who narrated from Yaḥyá ibn Sa'īd al-Qattān, who narrated from Abū Sa'īd Khalaf ibn Ḥabīb, who narrated from Anas ibn Mālik - may Allāh be pleased with him - that the Messenger of Allāh (ﷺ) said,

مَثَلُ هَذِهِ الدُّنْيَا مَثَلُ ثَوْبٍ شُقَّ مِنْ أَوَّلِهِ إِلَى آخِرِهِ، فَبَقِيَ مُتَعَلِّقًا بِخَيْطٍ فِي آخِرِهِ، فَيُوشِكُ ذَلِكَ الْخَيْطُ أَنْ يَنْقَطِعَ

"The example of this world is like a garment torn from end to end, with only a thread remaining at its edge. Soon, that thread will be severed."

If one would like further clarification regarding this example, look at what Aḥmad narrated in his *Musnad* from the ḥadīth of Abū Nadrah, from Abū Sa'īd, who said,

"The Messenger of Allāh prayed 'Asr prayer with us one day, then he stood up and delivered a sermon, mentioning everything that would happen until the Day of Judgment. Those who remembered, remembered, and those who have forgotten, have forgotten. People began to look at the sun to see how much of it (the day) remained.

He (ﷺ) then said, 'Indeed, there remains nothing of the world except as much as remains of your day from its beginning.'"

Ḥafs ibn Ghayyāth narrated from Layth, from al-Mughīrah ibn Ḥakim, from Ibn 'Umar, who said,

"The Messenger of Allāh (صَلَّى ٱللَّٰهُ عَلَيْهِ وَسَلَّمَ) came out to us while the sun was setting behind the palm trees and said,

'Nothing remains of the world except what remains of your day from its beginning.'"

Ibn Abī Dunyā narrated from Ibrāhīm ibn Sa'd, who narrated from Mūsá ibn Khalaf, who narrated from Qatādah, who narrated from Anas, that the Messenger of Allāh (صَلَّى ٱللَّٰهُ عَلَيْهِ وَسَلَّمَ) delivered a sermon at the time of sunset and said,

"Nothing remains of the world except what remains of your day from its beginning."

So, the whole world is like one day, and the Messenger of Allāh (صَلَّى ٱللَّٰهُ عَلَيْهِ وَسَلَّمَ) was sent in its last hours, just before its sun sets.

Jābir and Abū Huraira - may Allāh be pleased with them - reported that the Prophet (صَلَّى ٱللَّٰهُ عَلَيْهِ وَسَلَّمَ) said, while pointing with his index and middle fingers,

"I and the Final Hour are like these two fingers," and he put them together.[33]

Some of the Salaf used to say,

"Be patient, for these are just a few days. You are like travelers who are about to be called, and when one is called, he answers without looking back. Indeed, you have been informed about yourselves, and death is an inevitable departure. Allāh is watchful over you. The souls will depart, as has been detailed at the end of Sūrah al-Wāqi'ah."

---

33 Reported by *al-Bukhārī* (6505) and *Muslim* (867)

23. The world is like a large basin filled with water, made available to humans and animals alike. The water in the basin diminished due to the abundance of visitors until nothing remained except mud at its bottom, where animals urinated and both people and animals used to visit.

It is reported by Muslim in his *Ṣaḥiḥ* on the authority of 'Utbah ibn Ghazwān, who said in his sermon,

"Indeed, the world has elapsed and has turned its back. Nothing remains of it except a handful, like the handful of a vessel that its owner scoops. You are moving away from it to a permanent abode, so move with the best of what you have."[34]

Abdullāh ibn Mas'ūd said,

"Allāh has made the entire world small, and only a little of that small world remains. What remains of it is like a body of water whose pure water has been swallowed, and what remains is the muddy portion."[35]

24. A people inhabited a city for a period of time. During their stay, the city experienced numerous calamities and disasters, and its streets witnessed trials and invasions by troops of oppression and corruption.

Their king built another city in a location untouched by calamity or affliction. He resolved to destroy the first city and sent word to its inhabitants, commanding them to depart after three days, with no one remaining behind. He ordered them to move to the

34 Reported in *Muslim* (2967)
35 Reported in *al-Bukhārī* (2964)

king's other city, and that they should take the most beneficial and valuable items with them including pearls, gold, silver, and other items that could be carried and were considered highly valuable and suitable for kings.

He provided the guides and the means of transportation to facilitate their journey, erected flags to guide them, and appointed messengers to encourage them to hurry, each messenger following after the previous one.

The people divided into groups; the wise among them recognized the shortness of their stay in that city, and they were certain that if they did not hasten to acquire the best of what it offered and present it in the king's city, they would be unable to do so thereafter.

They saw it as unjust to spend their time gathering goods and being preoccupied with them, rather than seeking what was better. Thus, they inquired about the best things in the city, and those most beloved to the king and beneficial to his city. When they became aware of them, they did not turn their attention to anything less. They realized that when one of them presented a great jewel, it was more beloved to the king than if he presented loads of money, iron, or the like. Thus, their concern was to acquire what was dearest to the king and most valuable to him, even if it was less in the eyes of the observer.

Another group focused on loading the goods, and they competed in their abundance. Some had loads worth thousands, while others had less, depending on their ambitions and capabilities. Their concern was solely to load the goods and migrate from the city.

Another group focused on building palaces in that city and enjoying its pleasures. They opposed those determined to migrate and said,

"We will not allow you to take any of our goods. If you share in building the city and settling in it, we will live with you and share in it. Otherwise, we will not allow you to migrate, nor will we allow you to take anything from our goods."

A war broke out between them; they fought against those trying to migrate and seized their wealth and families. They only punished those seeking to migrate because of their departure to the king's city, responding to the caller and desiring the return to that city whenever he (the king) commanded them to leave it.

Another group who focused on leisure, idleness, rest, and comfort said,

"We will not tire ourselves in building or moving from here. We will also not oppose those who want to migrate, nor will we fight them or assist them."

The king had a palace there with female members of his family in a restricted chamber, surrounded by a wall and guarded by soldiers. The people of the city were forbidden from approaching it.

Those who remained in the city wanted to enter the restricted chamber, so they circled around it, but found no entrance. They approached the walls, dug under them, and reached the chamber. When they finally entered it, they corrupted and spoiled the woman, enraged the king, and caused him much grief. They also invited others to partake in their actions.

While they were in this state, suddenly a call was made, and none of them could lag behind. They gathering what they had and presented themselves before the king.[36] He reviewed them one by one, examining their goods and what they had brought from that (the old) city. He accepted from them what suited him, and generously rewarded their owners multiple times its value, and brought them close to his residence.

Others, he rejected what didn't suit him, and through it back in the faces of those who brought it.

He severally punished those who breached his sanctuary and spoiled the residence with the retribution they deserved. They requested permission to return to the city to rebuild his palace, protect his women, and present goods to him, similar to what the other merchants had brought. He replied,

"Never! The city has been ruined beyond repair, never to be rebuilt again. There is no city left after it except this city that will never be ruined."

36 What's apparent is that everyone had to travel in order to visit the king in the new city. (T.N.)

Various (short) Parables[37]

- The world has been likened to a dream and living in it is like being in a dream, while death is awakening.

- It has been likened to a farm and working in it is like sowing and harvesting is on the Day of Judgment.

- It has been likened to a house with two doors, one through which people enter, and one through which they exit.

- It has been likened to a snake, soft to the touch, beautiful in color, but deadly in its bite.

- It has been likened to poisoned food, delicious in taste and pleasant in smell. Whoever consumes it in moderation finds healing, but whoever exceeds their need finds death.

- It has been likened to food in the stomach; when the organs take what they need from it, withholding it becomes harmful or toxic, and there is no relief for its owner except in its elimination, as indicated by the Prophet (ﷺ) in the parable of the animals that eat green grass, as has proceeded.

- It has been likened to a woman among the ugliest of women, covering her eyes, deceiving people, and inviting them to her home. When they respond, she reveals herself to them, slaughters them with her knives, and throws them into pits. She has been granted power over her lovers to do as she wishes, both in the past and the present. It is astonishing that her lovers see their

37 The publisher added this title for clarity. (P.N.)

brothers being destroyed, yet they continue to compete in destruction, (as Allāh stated in the Qur'ān),

وَسَكَنتُمْ فِي مَسَاكِنِ الَّذِينَ ظَلَمُوا أَنفُسَهُمْ وَتَبَيَّنَ
لَكُمْ كَيْفَ فَعَلْنَا بِهِمْ وَضَرَبْنَا لَكُمُ الْأَمْثَالَ

{And you dwelled in the homes of those who wronged themselves, and it became clear to you how We dealt with them, and We set forth examples for you.} Sūrah Ibrāhīm: 45

What Allāh has mentioned in His Book is sufficient in illustrating it (the dangers of this life), and it is in accordance with its reality.

In another section of the treatise, the author mentions the following clarification,

"In reality, the world itself is not to be condemned, but rather the actions of a person within it are what deserve blame. The world is a bridge and passageway to either Paradise or Hell. However, when it becomes dominated by desires, personal interests, heedlessness, and turning away from Allāh and the Hereafter, these qualities become prevalent among its inhabitants and thus, it is associated with it. Consequently, it has acquired a negative reputation in general. Otherwise, it is the place for building and farming for the Hereafter. From it, provisions for Paradise are gathered, and within it, souls acquire faith, knowledge of Allāh, His love, and His remembrance, while seeking His pleasure. The best life enjoyed by the inhabitants of Paradise in Paradise was attained through what they cultivated in this world."[38]

The End of The Excerpts

38 Pg. 331, 332

Appendix[39]

How to use these Parables in Various Learning Settings

While translating these parables and reading them to community members in our local masjid, we also posted some of them on social media for others to benefit from. One day, a teacher from our online school commented that she could use these parables during her English lessons with her students. After careful thought, we came up with a few ways these parables can be used by Imams, school teachers, and even within the home among family members. We sincerely hope readers find these suggestions useful and we strongly encourage them to come up with more ways to benefit from these great parables mentioned by the author.

Suggestions for Masjids:

- These parables can be included in Friday khutbahs.
- They can also be read to the congregation after daily prayers and commented upon.
- These parables can be divided, printed, and posted on the masjid bulletin boards for worshippers to read, or copied and distributed for free reading.
- These parables can be posted on the masjid's social media platforms for the community and others to benefit from.

39 This appendix was prepared by the translator.

Suggestions for Families:

- Parents or guardians can read the longer parables to children as short fictional stories, and then explain the benefits to them.

- Families can read the parables together during their weekly learning circles, and then question each other on the benefits and lessons of each parable. Once children respond, parents can highlight other lessons that children possibly did not think of.

- In general, establishing a routine of regularly reading together as a family is important and helps to create a strong bond between family members.

Suggestions for School Teachers:

- **Reading Comprehension:** Have students read the parables and then answer questions about the main idea, themes, and characters. This can help improve their understanding and interpretation skills.

- **Discussion and Analysis:** Facilitate class discussions about the meanings and morals of the parables. Encourage students to share their interpretations and how the parables relate to their own lives or what they've witnessed or read about.

- **Creative Writing:** Ask students to write their own parables or stories with similar morals. This exercise can enhance their writing skills and creativity.

- **Role-Playing:** Have students act out the parables. This can make the lessons more engaging and help students better understand the characters and messages.

- **Comparative Analysis:** Compare the parables to other parables, to highlight similarities and differences in themes and storytelling techniques.

- **Vocabulary Building:** Use the parables to introduce and practice new vocabulary. Create exercises where students use the new words in sentences or find synonyms and antonyms.

- **Moral Reflection:** Assign reflective essays where students discuss the moral of the parable and how it applies to modern-day situations. This can help develop their critical thinking and ethical reasoning.

- **Illustration Projects:** Have students illustrate scenes from the parables. This can be a fun way to interpret and remember the stories visually.

- **Group Projects:** Assign group projects where students can create presentations or skits based on the parables. This encourages teamwork and deeper engagement with the material.

- By incorporating these activities, teachers can make the lessons more dynamic and foster a deeper appreciation for the wisdom conveyed through parables.

<u>*Notes*</u>

<u>*Notes*</u>

Made in the USA
Columbia, SC
28 May 2025

58552749R00036